MW00875314

Eyes Different Than Mine

By Erin Johnson

Illustrated by Isabella Muzljakovich

 FriesenPress

Suite 300 - 990 Fort St
Victoria, BC, V8V 3K2
Canada

www.friesenpress.com

Copyright © 2021 by Erin Johnson
First Edition — 2021

All rights reserved.

No part of this publication may be reproduced in any form, or by any means, electronic or mechanical, including photocopying, recording, or any information browsing, storage, or retrieval system, without permission in writing from FriesenPress.

ISBN
978-1-03-910547-8 (Hardcover)
978-1-03-910546-1 (Paperback)
978-1-03-910548-5 (eBook)

Juvenile Nonfiction, Social Topics, Special Needs

Distributed to the trade by The Ingram Book Company

Dedication

Dedicated to my brother, Matthew. Thank you for changing my world, opening my eyes, and being my best friend. And to my niece, Haylee -- I am so glad we get to share the role of being big sisters to our extra special siblings. It is the best gift.

Foreword: When raising a child with a disability, that child's siblings play a big role. Siblings share more with each other than anyone else in their lives -- their childhood, their physical features, their parents' attention, the focus of the family pictures hanging on the walls in their home. Siblings have the incredible privilege of growing up and experiencing so much of life together. They play, teach, argue, and forgive. When you are a sibling to an individual with a disability, all of these things remain true, but you also have unique elements included in your journey that are not so frequently acknowledged. You are no stranger to sacrificing for the sake of your brother or sister, you are well versed in patience, and you carry a depth of understanding that cannot be learned any other way. You fight for your sibling far more than you fight with them (which probably does happen, because you're siblings!). You are ready and willing to defend your sibling, educate others about who they are and what they need, and perhaps more than anyone else, you treat your sibling with the normalcy, dignity, and compassion you know that they deserve. You are both their family and friend, and that role is unique to you alone!

I cuddled my brother
in my arms
and held him close to me.

I kissed his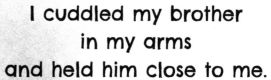
fingers and hands,
then opened them to see.

He had a crease across his palm,

so different from my hand.

But everything about this child
was just how God had planned.

I gazed into his eyes
while holding him that day.

They looked like little almonds
shaped in a
special way.

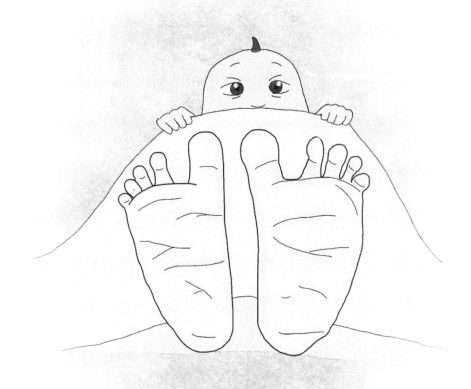

In between his first two toes
there was an empty space.

It seemed to me another toe
could fit right in its place!

My mom and dad loved him so much;
their hearts were full of joy.

They knew that God had given them an
extra special boy.

We knew our lives would change,
but all would be just fine.

I loved my baby brother

With eyes different than mine.

He'd snuggle in his blankets;
I loved to watch him sleep.

I wondered what he **dreamed** about,
Puppies, kittens, or sheep?

When he woke up, he'd look at me
with a **smile** on his face.

Smiles were a sister's job—
no one else could take my place.

We had a lot of helpers
who came to visit him at home.

Soon he **learned** to eat and crawl,
and walk all on his own.

My brother used his hands to talk;

he struggled with his **speech**.

He tried so hard to learn the words
that we would try to teach.

I'd take him to the playground,
we'd swing high on the swings.

And when I held him on the slide,
he'd flap his arms like wings.

The other kids would stare at him,
and some were so unkind.
But he would always smile at them,

With eyes different than mine.

My brother liked to do the splits--
his muscles made him **floppy**.

He touched his tongue to lick his chin,
a skill I tried to copy.

My **brother** joined a track team,
and he would run so fast.

He wore a smile on his face,
though he was often last.

At school, he learned with other kids
who had a **special** need.

They all would learn at their own pace
to talk or write or read.

Sometimes he needed **extra** help,
and things could take a while.

But as I watched him do his **best**,
it always made me smile.

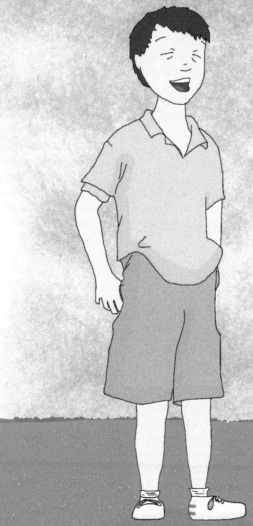

We sang a lot of goofy songs; the games we played were **loud.**

And everything about this boy would make me **very proud.**

As we've grown up together
he's become my closest friend.

He fills my heart with love and joy;
our bond will never end.

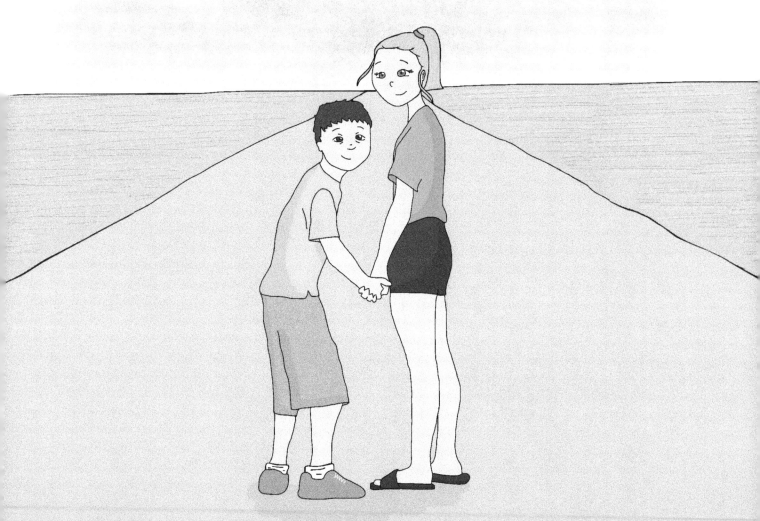

I've learned from my brother
that not all people are the same.

But I can always **be a friend**
and learn a person's name.

It feels good to be included,
and my brother would agree.

There's so much **worth** in each of us,
when we take the time to see.

My brother shows me strength and love–
the best this world can find.
I love my brother and he loves me,

With eyes different than mine.

Author's Note:

When I was growing up with a younger brother with Down syndrome, I was always looking for connections to others who had a sibling with a disability. I wanted to feel understood in the present and hopeful about the future. One of the first places I looked was the bookshelf. My parents had books about parenting a child with Down syndrome, and there were a few children's books that displayed a character with a disability, but I was never able to find a single children's book that shared the perspective of a sibling. I wanted today's generation of siblings to, from a young age, have a book on their shelves that recognized their role, acknowledged their experience, and encouraged their journey. I wanted to create a book that offered them hope for the friendship they have to look forward to with their sibling with a disability, because there is truly nothing like it.

This book is written from my perspective as I grow from a child to an adult. I am 6 years older than my brother. At that young age, it was hard for me to make sense of his having a disability and understanding what Down syndrome meant, but one of the first things I noticed were his eyes -- shaped differently than mine. In my story, I share my innocent observations as a young child, my experiences as an adolescent, and my reflections as an adult growing up alongside a younger brother with Down syndrome in hopes that other siblings who have a brother or sister with a disability will see parts of their own story, too.

Erin is a special education teacher and disability advocate who enjoys writing to share her heart. Erin's younger brother, Matthew, has what she calls the gift of Down syndrome. Erin wrote this book in Matthew's honor with the hope that it would encourage other young siblings of a child with a disability to feel understood and embrace their special role. Growing up with Matthew, and continuing their friendship in adulthood, has brought Erin so many cherished memories, and she loves sharing the gift that her brother has been to her and countless others. Today, Erin lives with her husband and two children in Holland, Michigan. Her family is waiting on the adoption of their third child, a teenager with Down syndrome. They receive frequent visits from Matthew, as he has fully assumed the role of uncle and can't stand being away from his niece and nephew for too long. He and Erin continue to be best friends.

Isabella is Kalamazoo-based artist. She grew up in the southwest suburbs of Chicago with her three siblings and parents. Isabella has always had a passion and love for the arts, and she was honored when asked to illustrate Erin and Matthew's story. Currently, Isabella is married to her husband, and they have two kids. Isabella is a stay-at-home mom who runs an Etsy shop on the side. When she is not busy creating, she enjoys spending time with her family and friends, traveling to warm places, and running!

CPSIA information can be obtained
at www.ICGtesting.com
Printed in the USA
BVHW020206160821
614493BV00006B/224

9 781039 105478